HOW TO DOMI

PROPERTY INV

IN THE UK

AND ACHIEVE FINANCIAL FREEDOM

BY

RICHARD ALVEN

www.propertyinvestinguk.com

While the author has used his best efforts in preparing this book, he makes no representation or warranty with respect to the accuracy or completeness of the contents of this book and specifically disclaims any implied warranties of merchantability or fitness for a particular purpose. No warranty may be created or extended by sales representatives or written sales materials. The advice and strategies contained herein may not be suitable for your situation. The author is not engaged in rendering professional services, and you should consult with a professional where appropriate. The author shall not be liable for any loss of profit or any other commercial damages, including but not limited to special, consequential, or other damages.

Table Of Contents

PLEASE CONTACT ME

Thank you very much for buying this book. I hope you enjoy reading it as much as I have enjoyed writing it.

If you have any questions on any of the material in this book, please get in touch by going to

http://propertyinvestinguk.com/contact-us/

Thank you

Richard Alven

GET OUR FREE NEWSLETTER

If you wish to receive our free newsletter and keep up to date with all the latest news affecting UK property investors then go right now to www.propertyinvestinguk.com and sign up.

This newsletter will contain any important new legislation which could affect you as an investor or a landlord. It will also provide details of any new investing hotspots in the UK and will update you on where about in the UK property prices are rising and falling.

So Don't Delay. Sign up now at www.propertyinvestinguk.com and keep abreast of all the latest developments.

PLEASE REVIEW THIS BOOK

Thank you very much for purchasing this book.

Please take the time to review this book on Amazon. I value all feedback.

Thank you so much and happy investing.

Richard Alven

INTRODUCTION

This book is a practical guide on how you can make money in property. If you have ever read an academic text book (and I feel your pain if you have) then you will know it contains all this nice theory but very little in practical explanation. You may also have read property books like this which go on about theory and how property is great and so on and on but do not give very clear direction in what to do.

It is for this reason that I have wrote this book as I think there is no other book like this. I will give you very specific instructions in how to buy property at a price significantly below market value (BMV) by working through an example with you using the Rightmove website. As we work through an example together you can go online and do the same process in your chosen location. It is so simple that a 5 year old reading this book and following the instructions will find a BMV property. It really is that easy, and it's the belief that this is a complicated process which causes people to lack confidence in their own judgment and pass up on amazing opportunities.

I have called this book "How to Dominate Property Investing in the UK and achieve Financial Freedom". In case anyone is wondering what I mean by "financial freedom", this is where you have a steady passive income coming in which more than meets all your expenses. You never have to work again and are therefore free to live the life you want to live. Does this sound appealing to you? Wouldn't you like to wake up one day and know that you don't have to go to work. Instead you can do whatever it is you want to do, whether that be travelling round the world, indulging in your favourite sport and hobby – whatever.

The unfortunate fact is however, that most people do not achieve financial freedom in their lifetimes. They work for 40 years to get a paycheck and after that they retire and survive on a pension. This is

7

not what I wanted for myself and was the key motivator in me looking elsewhere for income other than a salary. My father always said that you should "work to live" and not "live to work" and I agree with that except I understand now that there is no reason for having to work at all if you are financially free.

Becoming financial free is not that difficult either – not if you know what to invest in and how to invest in them. The answer to that is in this book. It is my estimation that if you buy just 5 of the properties that I recommend in this book, in the locations that I recommend you buy them in, then you will be financially free. As I will discuss in Chapter 1, property is probably the safest and easiest way to achieve your financial freedom.

So what I am going to cover in this book? Well, first of all I will show you where to invest. The bad news is that some places in the UK are far better to invest in than others and the place you live in now may not be the best place to buy property. Anyone who tells you that the best place to invest is in your own town is probably just lucky enough to live somewhere which is a good place to invest. The good news is though that the most desirable places to invest are likely not that far away. I will describe to you what these places are.

We will then talk about what types of property you should look for. With my strategy there is only one type of property and this keeps thing simple. I will also discuss what tools I use to help in my selection and evaluation process and I will share these with you.

Next, we will do a walkthough together of the process I use to find BMV properties so that you have the knowledge and the confidence to do this for yourself. I spent so much time learning this process with trial and error so this chapter really has lots of value for you.

The book then discusses the property viewing process, i.e. what to look for and what questions to ask the estate agent. Before you put an offer in on a property, you will want to find out as much as you can about the property and the person who is selling the property so this chapter will identity the kind of questions you should be asking the estate agent.

I will briefly touch on mortgages and solicitors but not go into too much detail as quite frankly it is as boring to read about as it is to write about. I will cover the things you need to know though.

Being a successful property investor is not just about buying properties but how to properly manage them. Therefore there is a chapter dedicated to discussing the things you need to consider once the purchase of the property has completed and you are now the landlord.

Finally I will discuss the strategy that I use for property investment – this is a strategy where you can have your cake and eat it – you will know what I am talking about when you read this chapter.

So without further ado, let's get started…..

CHAPTER 1 - WHY PROPERTY?

I have been investing in property for many years and this is where I have made and store my wealth. I have other investments, in stocks and managed accounts, but property is where I invest the vast majority of my money. The reasons I do this are threefold:

1   I am a conservative investor and I believe the property market to be safe relative to the stock market and other investment vehicles;

2   I can utilize leverage in my property investing , which enables my properties to outperform my other investments;

3   I understand property.

Let me expand on this:

Property is a physical asset. You can tell it has value just by looking at it. Look at the place you live in – it will have walls, floors, ceilings, windows, doors etc. All these things have value – as I am sure you noticed when you paid for them (or leased them). As long as you are living in a habitable environment then no-one can say that the property you live in does not have any value – you know it and so does everyone else, and they know it just by looking at it. You could look at a property that you know nothing about, and you would instantly know it was worth something (unless it had a serious problem such as termites, but let's be optimistic).

Let us look now at a share certificate. If I were to present you with share certificates of a publicly traded company that you never heard of before, would you instantly know what the certificates were worth? No, you wouldn't. You would have to do some research to see what the share price was at that moment in time to see the value of what you were holding in your hand. Once you know this value though, would you know what the value would be tomorrow? Again, no you wouldn't. The share markets go up and down like a roller coaster and share certificates that are worth £100,000 today could be worth £70,000 tomorrow and then £130,000 the next day. Also, the share certificates could be worth next to nothing if the stock market were to suddenly suspend trading on this share. The point I am trying to make is, it is impossible to know even approximately what a share certificate is worth just by looking at it (or even if it has any value at all), and it is impossible to know what it is going to be worth in the future – even if you were a Wall Street wizard. The share certificates themselves have no physical value except for the cost of some paper and ink.

With property, you can get a good idea of what a piece of property is worth by just doing a little bit of research. Property is much more stable than the stock market also, so if you have a property worth £100,000 today the chances are it will be worth £100,000 tomorrow. I therefore have confidence that if I were to put my wealth into property and invest wisely (if you follow the methods in this book then you will invest wisely also) then I will retain my wealth and not lose it during the next stock market crash. The housing market can also crash and indeed it did so in 2008/09, as it tends to do every 10 or 15 years or thereabouts, but the overall trend for the housing markets is an upward trajectory – always has and always should be.

Don't take my word for it though – look at banks and building societies. They are always advertising mortgage products, i.e. they are in the business of lending money so that you can purchase property. They do this because they know that property has value and they can secure the loan on this. Have you ever tried to ask a bank for a loan so that you can invest in the stock market? The bank manager would be rolling on the floor laughing if you did. Banks will not lend you money to invest in shares because it is too risky. It might be hard to believe but bank managers aren't all that stupid and they will only lend when they know they will get their money back from their loan. However banks lend money to buy property all the time, and it is one of the core parts of their business. They will gladly lend on property since property is a stable and sound investment as I mentioned above.

The fact that banks will lend you money to buy property gives you leverage and this is what makes investing in property so much better than investing in stocks and shares.

OK, so let's say you have £100,000 to invest but you can't decide whether you will invest this entirely in the stock market, or entirely in property.

If you had £100,000 to invest in the stock market, what value of stocks and shares could you get with this money? The answer, you might not be surprised to hear, is £100,000. £1 of your money will buy £1 worth of shares. No surprises there then.

However if you decided to invest in property, what value of property could you get for your £100,000. Some of you might be thinking £100,000 but there are two reasons why you would be wrong and this is because of leverage and illiquidity.

Let's assume therefore that the bank will lend you 75% of the purchase price of the property whilst you put up the deposit of 25%. Let us also assume that the bank will lend you 0% to buy shares. So with your £100,000 you will be able to purchase £100,000 worth of shares. However, what value of property can you buy with £100,000. Well since you only need to put up 25% of the purchase price you can buy properties worth £400,000 (£100,000 / 25%). Quite a bit better isn't it.

Now let's assume it's a year later. The stock market has risen 10% so if you invested in shares then you now have a portfolio worth £110,000. Pretty simple.

The property market however has risen by just 5%. At first glance it would seem that the stock market has done better and many financial commentators would write articles saying just that. They would be wrong though wouldn't they if you used the leverage available to you when purchasing property. If you used leverage to obtain a portfolio worth £400,000 with your £100,000, then if your portfolio of properties rose by 5% then your portfolio would be worth £420,000 – an increase of £20,000!! Compare this to the investment in stocks which rose by only £10,000. Now do you see how leverage can really improve your investment?

Some of you who are familiar with leverage might now be saying "Yes but leverage can increase the level of your loss as well as your gain". This is true, but I am not concerned with this in the property market. As I said earlier property is a stable investment and does not fluctuate widely year on year. I am also convinced that property will continue to rise in the long term, so leverage will be something which will help you, not hinder you.

We shall now turn our attention to liquidity, or rather illiquidity. Before we start I should probably define what liquidity and illiquidity means. A liquid asset is something that is, or can become cash very quickly. The most liquid asset is of course cash. Other examples would be a term deposit, or money owed to you by a good debtor and you know it will be paid shorty. An illiquid asset is something that cannot be turned into cash quickly and property would fall into this classification. It can take a long time for somebody to sell their house and if they wish to sell quickly (and in doing so receive nice liquid cash) then they may need to accept a lower price for their property.

So how does this help us? In the example above, I said that you could buy £400,000 worth of property with your £100,000. I said this to make the point I was trying to make as simple as possible but it wasn't entirely true. The price that people put their house on the market does not always equate to what I would call the fair value. As

13

I'm sure you will be aware, sellers sometimes put their property on their market with an asking price well in excess of what any right minded person would pay for it. If you were to buy properties such as this at the full asking price then your £100,000 would not buy you a property portfolio worth £400,000 – even with the 75% loan to value mortgage. The portfolio would be worth much less than that.

However the seller may put their property on the market with an asking price below what the fair market value is and it is these properties that I will be teaching you how to buy in this book. When you buy these properties below market value ("BMV"), then the value of the property portfolio you will be able to obtain will be well in excess of £400,000. I normally purchase properties at 30% BMV so if we apply that discount to this example then the value of the portfolio I could obtain with £100,000 would be around £570,000.

It is because of illiquidity that we can do this. The fact that properties are illiquid means that people are unsure what their property is really worth – even valuation experts cannot be 100% sure, and this means that their asking prices may not equate with their fair value – you can take advantage of this.

Illiquidity also acts as a motivating force for those who need liquid assets to sell quickly. To sell quickly they will likely need to put the property on the market at a price below the fair value. You can take advantage of this also. People need to sell quickly for a variety of reasons – perhaps the homeowners are getting divorced, or they want to move to another geographical location for work reasons and want the sale to complete before they move. Whatever the reason, properties with a motivated seller are on the market all the time.

I mentioned above the upward trajectory of the housing market. Have a look at this graph here:

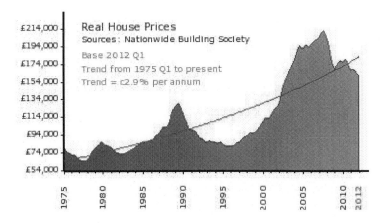

This graph shows the average house prices in the UK for the past 4 decades. You will notice that although there are peaks and troughs similar to a stock market chart, the overall trend is for the price of property to go up. There may well be crashes along the way but the price of property in the UK will always go up in my opinion. Look at the trend line on the graph and you will see what I mean.

This is what makes property such a great investment and yet I am surprised that so many people invest in shares yet so little invest in property. Imagine there was a company whose share price was always trending upwards. There might be short term rises and falls but the trend was always going upwards and you were 99% certain that it would continue to do so. Would you not invest in this company? I know I would. Well this is how I feel about property. I am certain that property will continue its upward trend in the UK and because of this, how can I lose? I've been doing this for years and I continue to win.

You might have noticed that I said above "I am certain that property will continue its upward trend in the UK". I do not believe that this holds true for every country.

For example, I currently live on a small Island in the Atlantic Ocean. It has a population of about 65,000 people and until a few years ago, had about 14,000 expats working and living there. Most of these people worked in the financial services sector. In 2008 the full effects of the recession was being felt around the world and the financial services sector was the first industry to really be hit. The Island's largest industry is financial services and so many expat workers lost their jobs and are continuing to do so six years later. As the population of the island continues to decrease by an alarming percentage, local property owners are seeing the value of their properties go down down down in value. If these expat workers do not return to the island in their droves then the property market here will be permanently marked down.

This will not happen in the UK. The UK does not have such a reliance on expat workers and it does not place great reliance in any one industry. The population of the UK continues to increase year after year and there is less and less space to build properties onto (it is not a big Island). Because they are cash strapped, the Government is not building many homes anymore and this is exacerbating the situation. Basic economics dictates that as the supply of homes decreases and the population increases, then there is going to be upward pressure on property prices.

It is my belief than in the next 20 years or so, people will realise the severe housing crisis that the UK is in and this upward trend is going to get steeper and steeper. Anyone who has the ability to own property will be very wealthy indeed, but this will be an achievement in itself and the vast majority of people will not be able to afford a home. I am actually starting to see this now. Spend 5 minutes browsing the website below and you will see what I mean.

http://www.shelter.org.uk/

You may have gathered by now that my strategy is one of capital appreciation – I make money by the value of my properties rising. In contrast to this, some people rely on an income strategy – they buy properties, rent them out and live off the rental income. Nothing really wrong with this strategy, but it's not what I talk about in this book. I do try to maximise rental income but only so I have enough money coming in to pay the mortgage and other expenses to continue to own the property. Any excess of rental income over property expenses is a bonus to me. I'm in this for the big money and a rental income strategy won't provide me the money that capital appreciation gives me.

But for capital appreciation to hold true, we need to invest in the right towns. So what towns are these?

CHAPTER 2 - WHERE TO BUY

Seaside Towns

There it is in 2 words. It took me years to find this out and I spent countless hours on the internet calculating yields (rental income relative to property values) to make this determination.

First of all I looked at cities. I looked at London, I looked at cities in the North of England, I looked at cities in Scotland, I looked at cities in Wales, but I couldn't really make property work in these areas, or at least I couldn't make it work as well as I wanted it to work – I knew it could be better.

I then started looking at large towns – places with more than 100,000 people living there. Some of these worked and some didn't – I couldn't really work out a pattern at this stage.

Finally I moved on to smaller towns with a population between 20,000 and 100,000. Again some were working and some weren't so I was becoming frustrated since I didn't know why it was that only some worked – especially as the ones that did were scattered all across the UK.

I was looking at Weymouth when it hit me that seaside towns were places to invest. Weymouth was a place where the yields were excellent. I was not familiar with a lot of the other places where I could calculate great yields but I knew Weymouth as I spent a night there several years before and I was obviously aware that it was a coastal town. I got a map out and I started to look at all the places where I was calculating good yields. I almost fell of my chair as I saw they were all seaside towns!!! That was my eureka moment and the moment I knew I was going to be very successful at this. I'm not sure if you have had this feeling before but it is the best feeling in the world.

I'm not 100% sure why it is that the yields are so much better in these towns than others. This seems to be because a lot of people retire to these places. They sell their homes in the city and decide to live out the rest of their lives by renting in a seaside town perhaps.

The reasons aren't all that important though – the fact is that seaside towns work better for property and that is all you need to know.

So what do I mean by seaside towns? There is no exact science to this but hopefully by using common sense you will be able to separate out seaside towns by places that are merely next to the sea.

Newcastle is not a seaside town. Hull is not a seaside town either. Although they are by the sea, they are also large cities and there are loads of other factors which determine property values in these places other than the quality of their beaches. Because of their size, you would have too many properties to choose from anyway and this makes things difficult.

I grew up in a small village in the North of Scotland which was by the sea. The population of this place is about 1,000 people. The place is known (if it is known at all) as a place of agriculture. There is a beach there but not many people know about it and those that do wouldn't even think about lying in on its seaweed covered surface. Again this is not a seaside town.

Brighton is a seaside town. Although it has a large population and is technically a city – it is considered by most people to be a seaside town (and it is "most people" who make up markets and ultimately determine what property values are - this falls under consumer psychology however and is outside the scope of this book). Brighton is known for its beaches, its pier, its arcades, fish and chip shops, ice cream shops and all the other things that seaside towns have in abundance.

If you need a helping hand then have a look at this Wikipedia page

http://en.wikipedia.org/wiki/Seaside_town#British_seaside_resorts

Hopefully you will be able to determine what is and what isn't a seaside town with relative ease.

The place you choose though should be of a certain size. Consider this hypothetical example of a seaside town which we will call Brightpool. Brightpool has everything a seaside town should have. It has all the stuff that I mentioned Brighton as having and even has a tower right by the beach. The one thing that Brightpool does not have though is many people – it has a population of only 1,000. As such there are not many Brightpool properties on the market at any one time and when there is, they are snapped up by one of the thousands of people who want to settle down in Brightpool. As such the property values are rather high (law of supply and demand – when supply is low and demand is high – prices rise) and it will be difficult to find a bargain. You will be competing with a lot of other people to buy available properties.

Ideally the population of the town you invest in should be at least 20,000. This means there should be enough properties on sale at any one time to satisfy normal demand and keep prices affordable. I talked earlier about liquidity, well financial people talk about liquid markets – this is when a market is large enough that no-one market participant can significantly alter the market by selling or buying in bulk. Going back to our Brightpool example, let's say a billionaire wanted to move his entire extended family there and made inquiries not only on the properties on the market, but even by convincing people who had not planned on selling, to sell. More residents would then be encouraged to sell at high prices and the billionaire would have significantly altered the property market in Brightpool. Although this example is slightly absurd, it does illustrate how external factors can easily affect prices in a small place. This does not happen so easily in larger towns.

But I don't live in a seaside town you maybe asking. Well, neither do I. The good thing about the UK though is that it is quite a small Island and seaside towns are never far away. Those of you who do not travel much may not think so, but believe me it is. There is almost certainly a seaside town that is within about an hour's drive from where you are. According to the Ordinance Survey, the place that is furthest away from the sea in the UK is a village called Coton in the Elms in Debryshire. It is 70 miles away from the nearest coast. Even residents of this village could see the great blue in about 2 hours by car. And even if is far then so what. Stay at a Bed and Breakfast and make a weekend out of it as you view your properties.

If the place where you will invest is not where you live, then it is wise to do some research on the place – especially if you have never been there before. First of all, do a search on Wikipedia so that you get general knowledge on the town and then have a look at the local newspapers for the town online.

You will want to get a good idea of what the place is like. You don't want a town that has a nuclear reactor for example so it is good to get some basic knowledge.

Google Street View

Use Google Street View to "virtually walk" around the high street and along the beach. A quick guide for those of you who aren't familiar with Google Street View – go to Google maps and find your chosen town. Select the little orange man in the top left corner and drag him onto a location on the map.

You will now be in Street View mode and will see a panoramic 3D view of the street your little orange man is on. You can then use your directional keys or your mouse to travel around the town. Isn't modern technology wonderful?

OK, so as I said take a walk around. Get a feel for the place – would you like to live here? Do you think other people would?

Becoming an expert in your chosen town

I would recommend only investing in one town and then becoming a property expert in that town. The more places you invest, the more you have to learn so why put yourself through more learning than is necessary. If you concentrate on this one place you will build up your knowledge each time you look at property and you will then become more and more of an expert.

You may or may not have heard of a concept known as The Zulu Principle. The Zulu Principle is an investment guide written by Jim Slater who discovered that after reading an article on Zulus in a magazine, his wife knew a lot more about Zulus than he did. He thought about this for a while and came to the conclusion that if his wife read a bit more about Zulus and made a visit to South Africa then she could easily become a world authority on Zulus.

I want you to become a world authority on the types of property that I recommend you invest in (which I cover in the next chapter) in your chosen town.

If you were to spend more than 100 hours looking at the property in a certain town then you will know more about the property market there than 99.9% of the people who live there. You will be able to tell just by looking at a property, the price that it would likely sell for. By focusing on just the one property type in your town you will become a world authority. How can sellers, estate agents or competing buyers stand in your way when you are such an expert? How can you make a mistake in your investment decisions? You will be invincible and can the treat the property market in your chosen town as a gold mine. You will literally make a fortune!!

Which part of town?

OK, so now we know the towns to purchase property in, but let's get more specific.

We are going to look at where about in a town you should invest in. You can find a lovely property with a nice view in a practical location but if it's in the roughest part of town with no amenities close by then this could affect your ability to get a mortgage, your ability to source a suitable tenant and could adversely affect a surveyor's valuation.

I know somebody that recently bought their own house after years of living there and paying rent to the council. Like many people she took advantage a scheme whereby she could buy her own council house. Good for her you might say. Well no, not really. Some council estates are worse than others and the one she lived in was the worst council estate in the town if not the entire county. This place had an absolutely dreadful reputation and local residents would be frightened to go near it. Well anyway, this lady decided to put her house on the market about 5 years ago. I looked at the local listings recently and the house is still on the market - at about 40% less than the original asking price. If she had lived in one of the more desirable council estates then she would not be having this problem.

You will know the good and the bad areas in the place you live – everyone does. Think of the place with the worst reputation in your town. Would you consider investing your well earned money there? Probably not.

What happens though when you invest in a town that you know less about? Well the first thing would be to ask someone who lives there (not an estate agent as they will say what they want you to hear). If you cannot get reliable advice from a local then I am going to show you another way.

Go to this webpage:

http://acorn.caci.co.uk/

and click on the button "try now". From here you will be able to register your details and begin using this site. When you return to this website in the future, you will just need to login using your credentials.

Begin a search using the postcode of the property you are interested in. If you need help finding a postcode then use this website http://www.royalmail.com/postcode-finder and enter the address.

After you enter the postcode you will be taken to a classification webpage. This is the classification type of the postcode according to a certain scale. This scale is a geodemographic classification system put together by CACI Limited and is based on data collected by the census. The scale breaks down the UK population down into 5 categories, 17 groups and 56 types. Have a look at this table by following this link:

http://www.caci.co.uk/acorn2009/acornmap_ext.asp

In reality it is very unlikely that you will purchase an investment property in the Wealthy Achievers category – not with the property strategy that I propose in this book (I do hope though you will soon be purchasing your own property in this category if you don't currently live in such an area). The highest ranking type I have purchased in was type 17. Most of my properties are types 20, 21 and 22. Whenever I find a property online that I am considering

24

viewing, I want to see where it lies on this scale. I have chosen a cut off at Type 36 so that I only purchase properties within the top 3 categories, i.e. "Wealthy Achievers", "Urban Prosperity" and" Comfortably Off". In other words I would only buy where the type is 36 or better on the scale.

The property types 37-56 will likely not be well served in a seaside town, or if they are, it will not be (as a rule of thumb) a desirable area to invest in. Please do not be offended with what I am saying here if you currently live in such a type. I grew up in a postcode classified as type 45 which is almost bottom of the scale but it is an area with good people and low crime. I would never invest there though.

I mentioned using Google Street View earlier to get an idea of the town you plan to invest in. Well once you have shortlisted a few houses you need to use this again to have a look at the street that your chosen property is in.

The estate agents photo of the property might look very nice but next door and the rest of the street might look hideous. I have also seen on Rightmove, a top floor flat for sale but the estate agents photo was of a ground floor flat. When I went on Google Street View I could see why – it looked like a fire had recently scorched the entire outside of the top floor. Whether this happened or not I couldn't tell but I certainly wouldn't want to invest in such a property.

So go on to Google Street View and have a virtual wander. You might want to "walk around" the other streets in the area and see what amenities are nearby. Almost everywhere is covered by the Google Street View Camera these days so there is virtually no limit where you can go to.

Imagine you are a surveyor and you are heading to the flat to make an official valuation. What are your impressions of the street? Do the houses look clean? Are the gardens nice and kept tidy? These are the kind of things a surveyor will be thinking about even before he sees the flat.

Now look at the flat itself from the surveyor's point of view. Again look at the state of the building and the garden. Try and get feel for the place – how does the building compare with the other buildings in the street?

It is important to see how nice the other properties in the street are. If you are in a horrible area with graffiti and flats in a poor state of repair then the property you are looking at will likely suffer from regression. This is where the value of a property is negatively impacted by other properties in the area, and is common sense. It is one thing to buy a property at what you feel is well below market value but there could be a very good reason why it is on the market for such a low price.

The more you look at the housing market in your chosen town the more "feel" you will get for what something is worth. It will be instinct. By using the internet in the way above you will be able to get a gut feeling of what something is worth without leaving your computer. So using your gut feeling, what is your impression of the place? Do you think this could be a BMV property, or is the asking price low because there are obvious factors which make it so (state of the building or the neighbourhood perhaps).

Now repeat the "virtual walk" above but this time do it from the point of view of somebody living there – your prospective tenant.

First thing to look for is parking. Is there ample parking in the street? Perhaps the building has its own parking round area around the back which might be visible. Good parking facilities are a valued attribute to any property and will be high on your tenant's wish list.

How far will your tenant have to walk to the nearest convenience store? Although a convenience store (or any commercial property) right underneath the flat is undesirable, such a store within easy walking distance would be a plus for your tenant. They will not have far to go when they run out of milk and when they are buying the Sunday papers.

The tenant is looking for somewhere to live that is convenient. They are not as concerned as the surveyor might be with how the flat looks – especially from the outside. They want somewhere that is either close to their work or close to a railway station, and if they have a car then they want good parking. In short, they want a place that will help them in their day to day lives and will not add any more stress.

I should mention here, that all properties that you look at should be within walking distance of a railway station. You really don't want to invest in a property that is more than a mile from a railway station (less than 0.5 miles is a great bonus). If you use the Rightmove website you will notice that they tell how far the property is from a railway station on the main sales page – this is how important they feel it is to have a railway station close by. I personally was quite surprised when I learnt how critical it was, as I am someone who likes to walk. However it is irrelevant what I feel is important – the fact remains that potential tenants will look for this and surveyors will take this into account when valuing the property. The closer you are to a railway station (without living above them) the better.

This wraps up all I have to say on location, location, location. In the next chapter we will discuss what property type to buy to make the most profit.

CHAPTER 3 - WHAT TO BUY

The small ones are the best

I don't know if you have ever eaten peas directly from a pod, but if you have and you are like me, then you will probably like the smaller peas the best since they are the juiciest. I like my properties like I like my peas – small.

So therefore I recommend 1 bedroom flats. These are the properties that you will be able to squeeze the most profit from and it is these properties that I promote in this book. The strategy I talk about may work with 2 bedroom flats or bigger but it will be harder and the profit will be lower – so why make life difficult for yourself. There will be more than enough 1 bedroom flats in your chosen town without the need to look at anything else.

The yields are better on 1 bedroom flats as there is a higher rental demand for them. Young professionals and old retirees tend to go for these properties in their droves which pushes the rental income up and this means more money for you.

It is better in my opinion to focus on just one property type and then become an expert on those property types (using the Zulu principle that I mentioned earlier). Why become a moderate expert on two property types when you can become the ultimate expert on just one type. This also makes it easier when analyzing properties as throughout the whole property selection process you are continually comparing apples with apples with more apples. You aren't throwing in the occasional orange which would confuse things.

Keep it simple – at least as simple as you possibly can.

You may be wondering about studio flats since they are even smaller (and therefore juicer right?) Do I recommend buying those? Well yes and no. Studio flats are less stable than other property types and tend to go through the roller coaster price movement that I used to describe the stock market earlier. If you buy when the market is at the very bottom then you will get a good deal as the prices are very low at this point. However if you buy and then the market drops even further then the value of your flat will drop big time. Personally I can do without the headache.

Also, studio flats tend to vary in size quite a bit which makes comparing them somewhat difficult. The 1 bedroom flats that I look at tend to be roughly the same size. They have a small/medium bedroom with a small/medium size living room with a small bathroom and a small kitchen – not a significant difference between properties. With studios though I have seen flats where they have just knocked a wall in a 1 bedroom flat which separated the bedroom and a living room to give a very big living room and a large studio. I have also seen a studio where they have lumped everything into 1 room – i.e. you have a living room with a murphy bed, a kitchen in the corner and a toilet in a cupboard!! Remember what I said earlier about comparing apples with apples. Well when you look at studios you will be throwing bananas, oranges, and strawberries into the mix.

Properties to avoid

When you get a mortgage, your mortgage provider will make some restrictions on the property that they are willing to lend on. I will talk through the most common restrictions below and so these are the ones to stay away from:

- High rise flats. Any flat which is in a building with more than 4 floors in it will likely be frowned upon by a mortgage provider as it gives the impression that it is a tenement block. This is true even if the apartment is on the lower floors – it is the building as a whole that is being judged and not your flat.

- Flats in large blocks (more than 20 flats in a block). This is for similar reasons to the above – the mortgage provider feels that these types of flats are of lesser value and they may not lend on it.

- Ex-council flats. For the same reasons as above.

- Flats above commercial properties. Lenders may stipulate that they will not lend on any flat that is above a commercial property as it "cheapens" the building. I strongly agree with this one and would not recommend you invest in a property above a commercial property regardless of what your lender says. In such a case it might be hard to find a tenant when you have a pizza parlour below your flat and there is a constant smell of garlic wafting in through the windows. Pubs are a definite no no – especially on a karaoke night and even seemingly less offensive units such as a shop can be annoying with the beeping of the door as it opens and people loitering around outside. Stay clear.

- New build. Some lenders don't really like brand new properties – properties less than 3 years old. These will normally be part of a large development and with so many identical properties coming onto the market at the same time, it may be harder to find a suitable tenant and also the property value may be less than the developer anticipated. Lenders are aware of the increased risks surrounding new builds and are less likely to lend on them.

- Maisonettes (flats with 2 or more floors). Maisonettes are slightly unusual and lenders do not like anything that is even remotely unusual. They like plain old vanilla flats.

The important thing to learn and remember from all this is that you must play by the rules that the lender makes. It does not matter that you love the flat, it matters what lenders think of the flat. Luckily lenders love lending on 1 bedroom flats as they realize the profit potential on them but they are quite specific on what kind of 1 bedroom flats they will lend on, and the list above illustrates that.

The way I see it though is, the lender and you are partners with the same objective. You both want to make a good investment with your money. The lender adds a layer of protection around your investment with their rules as they prevent you from making a mistake. They will only lend on a property that has saleable and rentable value and so by following their stipulations you should be more comfortable with your purchase.

CHAPTER 4 - HOW TO FIND BMV PROPERTIES

Step by step guide to using Rightmove

So how do we look for the best properties?

I use the Rightmove website (www.rightmove.co.uk) to find properties. The site is very easy to use and has good filtering options so that you can find the properties you are looking for. It also seems to have far more properties than any other UK website that I have looked at.

Go to the Rightmove website right now and we will go through this together.

On the main page, type in the name of your chosen town and then click on the "For Sale" button. You will then be brought to a filtering page where you can make your selection.

On the "Search Radius" line, select "This area only". You have the option of expanding the search radius to up to 40 miles but we are only interested in properties in the town itself.

For "Property Type" select "Flats/apartments"

For "Number of Bedrooms" select minimum of 1, maximum of 1.

For "Price Range" select "No min" and "No max". You might be wondering why we are selecting "No max" since we are trying to find BMV properties. I will show you why shortly.

For "Retirement properties" select "Non-retirement only".

For "Shared ownership" select "Non-shared ownership ".

For "Added to site" select "Anytime".

There is a tick box which, if you click it, will include properties under offer and sold subject to completion. It is interesting to see such properties but that is for another time. For now leave it unchecked.

Now click on the "Find properties" button.

This will bring you to a list of properties but before we start looking at them we have some more filtering to do.

You will see a "Filter your results" panel on the left hand side. On this panel is a "Preowned & new homes" section. We are only interested in "Pre-owned homes" so click on that.

At the top right of the screen you will be able to sort these properties by Lowest Price, so do that.

Now scroll down to the very bottom of the screen to see how many pages of properties there are. There are 10 properties per page so if there are 300 properties that meet your criteria then there will be 30 pages.

What we want to do now is to get an idea of the median asking prices for this selection. So divide the total number of pages by 2 and then click on the page number this gives you. For example if there are 30 pages then if you divide this by 2 you will get 15 – click on page 15. This will give you a good idea (albeit using a very crude method) of the current asking prices for 1 bedroom properties in your town that meet your criteria. Write this number down as the properties on this page will be on the same street or nearby to the properties that you will be purchasing. You will not be putting an offer in on the properties on this page though as the sellers are asking for the full market value. You will only be buying BELOW market value.

So take the total number of pages in your selection again. Now divide this number by 10. In the example above we had 30 pages so when we divide by 10 we have 3. We are only going to look at the first 3 pages of our selection which will give us the lowest 10% of the properties by asking price.

It is within these pages that will we do our final bit of filtering so that we find our gem. Think of this whole process as panning for gold. We have a pan full of dirt but by filtering and filtering we get rid of anything that does meet our strategy or does not meet our standard or price. What we are left with is pure gold.

OK, so have a look through the properties that are remaining. You will find that although we only selected 1 bedroom flats, there will be some studio flats in here because the estate agents have posted these incorrectly onto Rightmove. Strike these from your list as these are not what you are looking for.

You might also see some shared-ownership and retirement homes in there as well so strike these from your list. After a while you will know a retirement home just by looking at the photo as they have a distinctive look about them.

From now on you are going to have to be a bit more subjective in your selection process and use your judgment. Use your instinct to help you here. If there are any properties that do not look very nice from the photo then reject them – your first impression is very important.

Look to see if the flat is above a commercial property. If it is then this is not suitable so move onto the next property.

If they pass the initial test then click on them to get some more information. Are they close to a railway station? Read the description – is there anything here which might put you off? Is there only 20 years left on the leasehold?

Side note: a leasehold is a rental agreement for an extended period of time. Instead of owning a flat outright you would have a lease on the property – usually for between 50 years and 150 years. Towards the end of this term (if you are still alive) you can renew the lease. You would lease the property from the person who held the "freehold" of the building that the flat dwelled in.

Have a look at the other photos for the property which will likely be interior shots (if there are no other photos then that is a bad sign). How does the property look? Does it look clean inside? Is the decoration awful? Does it look like it will need a lot of refurbishment? (we will discuss refurbishment in detail later).

Do this for each of the properties in our selection criteria. It is a good idea to have a notepad handy and make notes as you go along. Write down the pros and cons of each property from the information you can gleam from the website.

Use Google Street View to walk around the property and the street it is on. Use the webpage http://acorn.caci.co.uk/ to see where the property lies on the classification scale and eliminate anything below 36.

Make a list of all the properties that meet the criteria. You may only have one property (unlikely) or you may have twenty. However in the absence of anything unusual that is yet to be discovered such as termites or dry-rot, you now most likely have in your hand a list of Below Market Value properties.

These are the properties that you will want to evaluate and we'll discuss that in the next chapter.

CHAPTER 5 - EVALUATE THE DEALS

Using Zoopla to do a quick valuation

I am going to show you now a couple of online tools which I use to get make a determination on the value of a property I am looking at.

From the list of properties that you have found on Rightmove, find these flats on Zoopla (www.zoopla.co.uk) and select them (one at a time). Hopefully you will be able to get the postcode and flat numbers from Google Street View. Otherwise you may have to call the estate agent to ask. Once you have your address select the "Current Values" box and then click search.

You will see that Zoopla has estimated a value for these flats using proprietary algorithms. They have also made an estimate on the rental value of the property per calendar month. Probably most importantly – it will mention any recent sales and what the property sold for.

A word of warning however. These are very rough estimates that Zoopla are creating and should not be used in isolation. Here are a couple of real life examples to illustrate this point.

On one occasion I was on the brink of purchasing a property for £105,000 as I believed its true market value to be closer to £150,000. When I looked up the property on Zoopla I was very surprised to see that the property valuation figure they had was under £88,000. I researched further and found out that the last sale took place 2 years earlier for an amount of just £90,000. I couldn't believe that the price was so low and I must admit that I began to question my maths and my own judgment, given that I thought the true value to be so much higher.

In the end my instinct won, and I went ahead with the purchase for a price of £105,000 as I knew it was worth far more than that. As I went through the conveyancing process I found out that the present owner had purchased the property from her parents for £90,000. So at last the figure made sense – the parents had sold the property at a heavily discounted price to their 20 year old daughter to help her out.

I am looking right now at the Zoopla data for a flat I purchased a couple of years back. The current estimated value per the Zoopla estimate is just under £73,000. I am not sure how exactly the Zoopla algorithms work but I know they take into account the last sales price for the property and then adjust it for market conditions in the area. Before I bought this property the Zoopla estimate was £110,000. I then bought the property for £76,000 (significantly below market value) and the Zoopla estimate was revised at that time. At the time I purchased the property the Zoopla estimate was £76,000 and it has decreased steadily as market values continue to fall. I know that the fair market value is closer to the original estimate of £110,000.

The estimated rental value per Zoopla for this flat is £294 per calendar month. The actual rent I receive is £450 per calendar month. Again I am not sure how the algorithm works but I suspect it takes the estimate of the property value into account when estimating the rental value, and because I am buying significantly below market value then the rental value estimate is skewed downwards. Zoopla would therefore give the impression that the rent achievable on my property is a lot less than what I actually receive.

Again the Zoopla figures were skewed and I did well to trust my judgment in this case. This next technique though is much more reliable in my opinion. This is something I learned when I was studying finance as it is used to calculate the value of an income generating asset based on the income it receives.

So as I said Zoopla has calculated the rental value to be £294 per calendar month and the value of the property to be £73,000. Let's calculate the rental value multiplier by taking the property value and dividing the rental value per month.

$$\frac{£73,000}{£294} = 248.2993197$$

We take this multiplier and apply it to the rental income that I actually receive. I receive £450 per month and so £450 * 248.2993197 = £111,735.

Therefore Zoolpla's algorithm believes my property to be worth £111,735. I concur with this valuation (looking at the asking prices of the 1 bedroom flats in the area) and believe that the true market value of my property is in this region. I have made an unrealized profit therefore of £35,735 since I purchased this property for £76,000.

So how does this help you when trying to find a property? Well, it will help you as we can now calculate with a high degree of certainty the value of a property by simply knowing what rent you can receive on it.

The ten step checklist

I have prepared a ten step checklist below to make sure you have covered all the required steps when evaluating a property:

1   What is the asking price for this property?

2   What is the median asking price for properties of this type and size in this town using the rightmove website?

3   How much more is the median asking price than the actual asking price for this property? (2 − 1)

4   What is the classification per the postcodeanywhere.co.uk website? Is it better than 36?

5   Have you done a "virtual walk" with Google Street View? Any points to note?

6   What does Zoopla estimate the property value to be?

7   What is the average rent per calendar month in this area using Rightmove?

8   What is the "Zoopla Multiplier" for a property type in this area?

9   What is the value per the Zoopla algorithm? (7 * 8)

10   How much more is the value per the Zoopla algorithm than the asking price for this property? (9-1)

I am objective person by nature so I like using maths to make decisions for me which is why I created the above 10 step checklist. If the values in rows 3 and 10 are high then there is a very good chance you have a property that is being offered at a price significantly below market value. Now look closely at rows 3 and 10 in the above checklist. Does this property still look appealing to you?

Of course you need to be subjective as well, as consider the state of the neighbourhood and more specifically the building and flat themselves, but before I get to that stage I like to use maths as much as possible to weed out properties that aren't up to scratch.

Complete this checklist for all properties that you are looking at. You can then compare them to see which might be the best properties to arrange a viewing for or to make an offer on.

This chapter and the previous chapter is, in essence, the key to dominating the property market in the UK. Very people have worked this out and those that do go on to make a lot of money. What's more you can do all this without leaving your armchair.

CHAPTER 6 - A WALKTHROUGH OF THE PROCESS

I will now perform a walkthrough of the entire selection process that I use to find Below Market Value properties. By doing so I believe I will show to you just how easy this really is. This entire process is done online.

I shall look for a BMV property in a town that I don't normally buy in – Brighton, and I know that at the end of it, I will have found a BMV property.

So let's get started…

I have done the initial filter as described above so that we are only looking for properties that are in Brighton itself, has 1 bedroom and is non-retirement.

When I click on "Find Properties" I am taken to the properties list. I will now filter out the auction and shared ownership properties and I am left with a list of 355 properties.

I will sort by "Lowest Price" and scroll down to the bottom to see how many pages there are. Since there are 355 properties, there are 36 pages.

To get an idea of the median asking price I will divide 36 by 2 to get 18, and go to the 18th page. The house prices on this page are all £165,000 so that is a good indication of the average asking price at the moment for 1 bedroom flats in Brighton. As I have said before this is a very crude method so don't place too much reliance on these prices.

I shall now filter further by only looking at the lowest 10% of the properties when sorted by asking price. 36 * 10% = 3.6 pages so therefore we will look at the first 4 pages in this selection.

The most expensive property on the 4th page is £130,000 so I am going to go onto the 5th page and look at the properties on that page that are £130,000 also.

On page 1, I am seeing a lot of beach huts – obviously these should be filtered out. I also see studio flats and retirement properties which I will take out as well.

The first flat on the list that meets my requirements is a flat for £115,000. The property looks quite nice from the outside so I will click on the property and look further:

Location is good as it is within half a mile of two railway stations. I have read the description and there is nothing in there which is causing me to believe that there is something wrong with the property.

The photos of the interior show a modern looking flat that is in need of little refurbishment – a professional clean is probably all that is required to make the property ready for a tenant.

I have done a virtual walk using Google Street View and the properties in the street all look similar to this one – all very clean and no red flags here.

Google Street View has given me an address. I will enter that into the Royal Mail website I mentioned earlier so that I can get the postcode:

http://www.royalmail.com/postcode-finder

With this postcode I can see where the property has been classified according to the classification system on http://acorn.caci.co.uk/.

This postcode has been classified as type 20 which is certainly acceptable to me.

Lets see what the Zoopla algorithms thinks the value is by using the multiplier valuation method I talked about earlier.

I will enter the postcode into Rightmove but instead of clicking on the "For Sale" button, I will click on the "To Rent" button.

I will look for 1 bedroom flats within ¼ mile area as it is unlikely that I will get a large selection of 1 bedroom properties to rent just in this postcode alone. I will leave the minimum and maximum price fields blank.

I now have a list of fifteen 1 bedroom flats with ¼ mile of my property. The rental values range from £625 per month to £775. There are more properties above £700 than below so I think the average price is slightly above £700. Let's be conservative though and say the average rental value is £700 per calendar month.

Now we shall go to the Zoopla to find our multiplier for 1 bedroom flats for the area.

I have entered the postcode into the search box and selected "Current values" as before. From this list I have found a comparable property (a 1 bedroom flat) and I have selected it.

The rental value for this flat is £600 per calendar month and the property value is £140,000.

The multiplier is therefore:

£140,000

£600   =   233.33334

When applying this multiplier to our average rental of £700 above, we get an estimated value of £163,333.

So Zoopla's algorithm "believes" that the value of the property I looked at earlier with an asking price of £115,000 has a value of £163,333.

I have now added this property to my shortlist and I will repeat for all the properties up until the £130,000 asking price.

Do you see how easy it is to find Below Market Value properties? In 5 minutes I have found a very good looking flat in a good location, in a good street for an asking price that is approximately £50,000 below the average asking price in that town. I will of course need to do a viewing of the property and have my solicitor review for any problems but I am certain that I have just found a nugget of gold. I am also certain that there will be plenty of more nuggets on the next few webpages.

Most people think it is extremely difficult to find BMV properties, but I have never had a problem here. If you know the process (and now you do) then it is extremely easy.

CHAPTER 7 - VIEWING THE PROPERTY

Once you have your list of BMV properties you will want to view them. The Estate Agents number will be on the Rightmove website so phone them up and arrange a time.

Either on this phone call or when they meet you – the estate agent will likely try and get you to view other properties that they have for sale. Unless you have the time to spare then my advice would be to politely decline. You have a shortlist of the best properties currently available for sale so why would you want to spend your time looking at these average properties?

On the day of the viewing it is a good idea to get there 15 – 30 minutes before so you can walk around the area to inspect the neighbourhood for real. Using Google Street View is good but it is no substitute for the real thing.

When dealing with an estate agent, the important thing to remember is to be yourself. I have heard a lot of people say that you need to need to act in a certain way with estate agents. Rubbish – just be yourself. This is not some covert operation, and you're not auditioning for theatre, all you are doing is buying a property. By saying you need to act this way or that way they are making the whole process seem more difficult than it really is. No wonder so few people buy property.

Once the estate agent arrives and lets you in to look around you will probably only spend about 5 minutes viewing the property. There will not be many rooms for you to inspect and so it will not take you long. You just want to get a general idea of what refurbishment will be needed (if any) and if there is any major damage to the property.

Have a look for any large cracks that could indicate a structural problem. Most cracks in an old flat are just superficial in nature but it is worth making a mental note of any and getting them checked out if you do end up putting an offer in.

If your memory is poor then feel free to take notes of what you see as you walk round. Personally I just store all my notes in my head and then put them to paper as soon I part company with the estate agent. Don't be afraid to take a note pad with you though and write as you view.

Regardless of when you make the notes, you will need to have at some point, notes on the general condition of the place, what needs repairing, what needs replacing, what needs cleaning. Once you view all the properties on your list then - all other things being equal - you will want the property that needs the least amount of work done to it. I did say "all other things being equal" so if you are looking at a property with a £115,000 asking price and it requires £3,000 to refurbish and you also look at a £117,000 that requires £2,000 to refurbish – then you might be better off with the £115,000 property since the total cost to bring it to your standard is lower in total (£118,000 vs £119,000). There are other things to consider though when comparing properties.

You will want to ask certain questions to the estate agent. I tend to ask my questions as I am walking round rather than interrogating them at the end of the viewing but whatever you feel more comfortable with. Again, you will want to write down the answers to these questions either during the viewing or shortly afterwards while it is fresh in your mind. Here are the questions that you should ask as a minimum:

- Why is the vendor selling? Is it because they are looking to move somewhere bigger or is it because the person in the flat below plays heavy metal music to 3am?

- How long has the property been on the market for? If it has been on the market for several months then the vendor may be open to negotiate the price.

- Do you know what the vendor's situation is? This is probably the most important question. By asking this, we want to know if the vendor is moving to a bigger house, or a different area perhaps, or if they are about to repossessed. If it is the latter then this obviously gives you some useful information when considering your offer.

An experienced estate agent will likely not give you any information which would work to your advantage at the expense of the seller (who they are working for) but not all the people who will show you round will be experienced. Showing people around properties is considered a bit of a pain for estate agents and so it normally gets delegated to junior staff with the senior staff getting involved if you make a serious offer. I would say about 75% of the time, it is a young person in their early to mid 20s who show me around a property and they quite often divulge more information than they probably should. This works to your advantage.

After you view the property and received answers to your questions, you should have enough information to make a decision on whether or not you will make an offer and if so what your offer will be.

47

CHAPTER 8 - HOW TO MAKE AN OFFER

Most people get very stressed when it comes to making an offer. I think there are probably 2 opposing reasons for this:

- They are worried that they will offend the vendor or the estate agent by putting in a ridiculously low offer.

- They are worried that they will make an offer in excess of what the vendor would accept.

Personally I am more concerned with reason no. 2, but if I am being strictly honest then they are both reasonable concerns.

You might hear some people say that you can never offer too low a price. To an extent I agree with this and it is certainly better to be bold and offer on the lower side. I would rather make the mistake of offering too low a price than too high as at least I can revise my offer upwards later (unless you have a good reason for doing so, such as something being wrong with the property, you can rarely revise your offer downwards).

Having said that, you don't want the estate agent to think you are an idiot. If you offer half the asking price for a property that already is below BMV then they will think you're stupid and might not deal with you. If they do deal with you it is unlikely that they will continue to take you seriously and may even try to take advantage of you.

I had a friend of mine who recently tried to sell his scooter. He thought it was worth about £1,000 so put it on the market for that price. He was amazed at the amount of people who came in with offers of £700 – £800, despite the fact that many of these people never even came to look at the bike.

I learned from this and so when it came time for me to sell my scooter I put it on the market for £1,000 even though I knew it was only worth £500 at the most. Sure enough I eventually got an offer of £700 from a person who hadn't even looked at the bike and sold it to him. I wasn't 100% sure the deal would go ahead once he actually saw my scooter but it did. He drove away on the scooter, happy as can be, thinking he got a bargain because he had no knowledge of the true value of the scooter. And because I knew this I took advantage.

The point I am trying to make is, if you make a ridiculously low offer, you might come across as clueless and estate agents may try and exploit you – if not with this property then another property they are trying to sell. I don't think this will happen to anyone reading this book since you are taking action to educate yourself on property, but it does happen to a lot of other people.

There is nothing worse though than offering too high a price. If you get your first offer accepted immediately then you will be kicking yourself for the rest of the day - it is not a good feeling.

When I first got started property investing in my chosen area, I was looking to purchase a property in the region of £105,000 as this was sufficiently below the average asking price of 1 bedroom flats in the town of about £145,000. I looked at this very nice flat with an asking price of £119,000 and considered making an offer of £105,000. In the end however I decided against it as I thought that making an offer £14,000 below the asking price was just too great and didn't want to embarrass myself. I knew that the property was repossessed and would therefore likely go for a lower price than would otherwise be the case, but still – I just couldn't believe that the property would go for anything less than £112,000 which was outside my price range.

Do you know what this property sold for in the end? This lovely, modern flat was finally sold for £95,000. I cannot repeat the words I used when I found this out but they were not pleasant. I remember being very angry at the person who managed to purchase the flat for that price - I was thinking "How dare he/she offer such a ridiculously low price for this place, what a cheek?" Now I think – kudos to them – they are were obviously a much better property investor than I was at the time.

Side Note: A repossessed property is one that has been reclaimed by the lender as the owner has not been able to pay the mortgage on this property.

There is no real correct answer to the question "How much below the asking price should I offer?" It really comes down to the vendor's situation, so the more questions you ask the estate agent about the vendor then the more information you will likely have to make a determination about what your offer should be.

Please remember though that if you follow my guidelines above on finding BMV properties then the asking prices will already be significantly below the fair value of the properties. For all the properties I have ever bought, even if they were bought at the asking price it still would have been a great deal. I will never put an offer in on a property that was not a great deal at the asking price although I have never had to pay the full asking price.

For those people who just cannot find out enough about the vendor then I will give you some rules of thumb that you could follow when making offers. If you do follow them then it is unlikely you will go far wrong and they are good guidelines for the investor just starting out:

- For repossessed properties, make an offer 20% less than the asking price and revise upwards in increments of £2k until you have a deal.

- For all other properties, make an offer 10% less than the asking price and revise upwards in increments of £1k until you have a deal.

I arrived at 20% and 10% because I tend to end up purchasing most of my repossessed properties at about 15% lower than the asking price and purchase most of my other properties at about 7% lower than the asking price.

As I said, these are just guidelines but if you follow them, along with following my advice on finding a property, then you will make better property investment decisions than 99% of everyone else.

I think I should point out though than when it comes to making offers on repossessed properties – even if the repossessing lender tentatively accepts your offer, they will continually seek higher offers until the deal is completed. There is an increased risk therefore of the deal not being completed.

CHAPTER 9 - THE PURCHASING PROCESS

I'm going to talk for a bit now on mortgages and solicitors – mainly mortgages. I could write a whole book on this but I am not going to for 3 reasons (i) it would be boring for me to write (ii) it would be boring for you to read, and (iii) the mortgage world is constantly changing with new products coming out all the time, so anything I mention here about the products available will already be out of date by the time you read this.

What I will discuss instead is the very general things you need to consider when taking out a mortgage.

Before I go on though, I should point out that I am not a financial adviser. What I am aiming to do in this chapter is to give you the benefit of my experience in using mortgages so that you may avoid some of the problems that I have faced. I do not know you or your personal circumstances which is why I try and keep my advice in this area very general. It could be that this advice may be wrong for you based on your own personal circumstances so if in doubt, please talk to a professional.

Background

The word mortgage means "death contract". This might be why so many people are scared of them. They are named such because the commitments and obligations under the mortgage agreement "die" when you either pay all the money back to the bank or you fail to keep up your payments and the bank repossess your property.

Mortgages are simply a loan from a lender to enable to purchase a property. The loan is secured on the property that you are buying. A bank will offer you a mortgage of a certain percentage of the purchase price of the property. For example they may give you a loan of 80% of the purchase price so that you have to finance the

20% yourself (the deposit). A loan of 80% would be termed 80% LTV where LTV stands for Loan To Value.

Mortgage Brokers

As I said above, the mortgage world is never constant and is always changing as new products are being offered. It is very difficult to keep on top of what mortgages are available if you do not work full time in this area.

I have had a look on a "mortgage broker only" website which had a list of literally 1,000s of products – all with their own little quirks and restrictions. Some had high rates, some had lower rates, some required a deposit of just 10% whilst other demanded more than 50%.

I also saw a product that offered pretty good terms, except it would only lend to properties bought in Ipswich. For whatever reason they didn't much like lending on any property anywhere else – and that's fine. Their money = their rules.

Anyway, the point is, it is going to be very difficult for you to know all the products that are available. It will be even more difficult to know of all the best products that are right for you. This is why you need a mortgage broker, and this is why you need a good mortgage broker.

A good mortgage product can make all the difference between a fantastic deal and a deal that is only average. It is very important that you get a suitable product as you could be making mortgage payments for a long time. The last thing you want is to be making payments that are higher than they need to be because you were not made aware of all the options available to you at the time you needed the mortgage product.

So how do you find a good mortgage broker? Well the first thing is, make sure they have access to all the lenders. Many brokers don't and so they will try and push you a product that may not be as good as others that are available.

Secondly, make sure that they have buy to let products available. There is a difference between mortgages available for owner occupiers and those available for property investors. Some brokers specialize in only one of these tranches.

Finally, it is very helpful that you have a broker that understands what you are trying to do. If you decide to follow the strategy espoused in this book (Chapter 12) then you will need a broker that will provide you with the best refinancing options to accommodate this strategy.

If you are researching brokers then make sure they you do your due diligence on them using the three points above.

There is one mortgage broker that I know meets all these requirements and they are called Connect Mortgages whose website link is below:

http://www.connectifa.co.uk/

They have access to all the buy to let lenders but most importantly, they have a good understanding of various investment strategies so can really help you here.

Repayment vs Interest Only

A repayment mortgage is a mortgage where you borrow a sum of money from a lender, and then when you make regular payments back to the lender, part of the amount you pay is interest on the mortgage, and the rest is a repayment of the principal amount lent.

At the end of the mortgage period (usually 25 years) you will have paid back the entire principal amount of the loan as well as all the interest accruing on this loan.

An interest only mortgage is one where, throughout the life of the mortgage, you only pay the interest. At the end of the mortgage period you will be required to pay back the entire principal amount in one go. So if you borrowed £100,000 and paid 8% interest on this, you would be paying £8,000 a year in interest and at the end of the mortgage period you will need to pay back the entire sum of £100,000.

I'm tempted to keep this section very short and just say go with interest only mortgages – take my word for it. But I have a feeling that this won't satisfy most of you.

The key reason why interest only mortgages are vastly superior is due to inflation and I think I can explain this best by using a real life example.

I have some friends who recently finished off paying their mortgage after 25 years. They bought their house in 1987 for the grand sum of £21,000. To them, back then, this was quite a bit of money considering their low wages and because they had chosen a repayment mortgage they were paying about £150 per month in the beginning – a sizeable chunk of their pay-packet. In fact after they had paid their mortgage, their bills and put food on the table for the family they only managed to save £10 per month. Life was not easy.

However, if they had taken an interest only mortgage they would have been paying back only about £100 per month. This extra £50 per month would have been a big help to them.

Anyway they went with repayment as they liked the idea of paying back the principal amount of their mortgage over the years so that there wouldn't have to pay back this amount in one lump sum at the end of the 25 years.

At the end of the 25 years though, the value of the property had increased to about £200,000. If they had chosen an interest only mortgage then they would have had to only pay back £21,000 at the end of the mortgage which was just over 1/10th of the value of the house. They could have paid this back easily with the amount of money they had at this time – and they wouldn't have had to struggle.

Or they could have released some equity in their house by refinancing it as it increased in value, which again, could have easily covered their existing mortgage.

When it comes to property investing, you have to keep your costs as low as possible and that includes your mortgage cost. Why make life more difficult for yourself by making monthly payments that are higher than they need to be. Always, and I mean always – go with an interest only mortgage.

Fixed Rate vs Variable Rate

A fixed rate mortgage is one where you pay interest at a fixed rate – the interest rate remains the same throughout the term of the mortgage.

A variable rate mortgage is one where the rate of interest varies in accordance with the market. The rate will likely be tied to an index, such as the Bank of England rate, and will fluctuate in accordance with that.

A very common question is whether you should take out a fixed or variable mortgage. This is an area where there is no clear cut answer and if you have a large portfolio of property (or intend to have a large portfolio of property) then it is a good idea to have both fixed and variable interest mortgages in your portfolio.

My properties are about 50% variable and 50% fixed. Right now my variable interest properties are doing better since Bank of England interest rates are at an all-time low. If these rates were to rise by just 3% then my fixed rate properties would be doing better.

Also, for your chosen mortgage product, compare rates of both fixed and variable to other currently available mortgage products. It could be that your product has a lower than average fixed rate but a higher than average variable rate, (or vice versa) in which case you might want to go with the fixed rate for this product.

Fixed rate mortgages tend to be more expensive than variable interest but by locking in your interest rate for a few years you have a degree of certainty that you would not have with a variable mortgage. It is therefore a kind of insurance.

As I said above, interest rates are currently at all-time low at the moment. Therefore I am currently taking out my mortgages on a variable interest basis. However, I pay close attention to the Bank of England meetings where they decide what the interest rate should be. There will be a day, and that day will come soon, where 2 or more of the board members will vote to increase the interest rate, and when that happens I will start to take out fixed rate mortgages on any new purchases that I make. It is my belief that when 2 or more board members vote this way then such an increase will not be too far away.

Solicitors

The definition of Conveyancing is "the transfer of legal title of property from one person to another". Therefore this is the process you must go through after you have agreed to purchase a property from a vendor but before the legal title passes to you. This is the part of the purchasing process which you will delegate to a solicitor.

A solicitor will check all the documents relating to the property and will bring to your attention any issues which could cause complications. One time I was in the process of purchasing a property but my solicitor discovered that the property would not be allowed to be let out. Obviously I could not go through with the purchase.

When I first started Property Investing, I thought it didn't really matter what solicitors to use. I therefore went with the cheapest solicitors I could find. My attitude towards this changed though when I was purchasing my second property. The solicitor was extremely slow in performing the work he needed to do and would not respond quickly to inquiries from either myself or the estate agent. The vendor was almost ready to walk away from the deal when finally the conveyancing process was completed and I got the property. I learned my lesson though and decided to not be so thrifty going forward.

You might have heard of the saying "You only get what you pay for". Now if you have been absorbing what I am telling you in this book then you will know that I don't believe in that saying when it comes to buying property. I do believe in it though when it comes to solicitors so don't be afraid to spend a bit more to get the better ones. Using the example above where I almost purchased a property that could not be let out – imagine the solicitor did not discover this and I bought this property which would have been useless to me. This is the value of having a good solicitor.

So what do you need to look for in a solicitor? First and foremost, they need to understand property and they need to understand your strategy. Ask for some recommendations if you know of other property investors in the area and use the internet to look for reviews of good solicitors.

If you use the mortgage broker that I recommend in this chapter, then you can use their solicitor and he is fantastic. He understands property and he understands the strategy I employ. If you decide not to use this mortgage broker then try and find a solicitor who meets the requirements above.

Recently I have also been using solicitors that are recommended by the estate agent I am purchasing the property from. I used to think this might be a conflict of interest and avoided doing this, but I have thought about this some more and have abandoned the idea that this might be a conflict for two reasons:

(i) Solicitors are highly regulated in the UK and have very strict independence requirements when it comes to their clients. Any breaches in independence are taken very seriously by the institutes which regulate the industry and solicitors are required not just to be independent but to be "seen to be independent:". It is very unlikely that a solicitors independence would be comprised in my opinion.

(ii) When a sale on a property has been agreed and the conveyancing process is under way, all parties involved (the seller, the seller's solicitor, the buyer, the buyer's solicitor, the estate agent, the mortgage lender and the mortgage broker) want the same thing. They want a smooth transition in ownership. Once I agree a price with a seller to purchase their property, then I view us all as being on the same side (unless there are problems with the property that were previously undisclosed, then I need to negotiate the price down some more). If we are all on the same side then what does it matter if the estate agent and my solicitor have a relationship.

59

There are also some advantages to using a solicitor recommended by the estate agent. If the conveyancing process drags on (as they often do) then this is normally because the sellers solicitor are dragging their feet or because your solicitor is dragging their. Quite often in my purchases I suspect that both solicitors are dragging their feet. In situations when the purchase is dragging on, it is difficult to ascertain which solicitor is to be blame and hence who needs chased up. When I have chased up my solicitor they always blame and the seller's solicitor and I am sure the seller's solicitor is blaming my solicitor to their clients. The estate agent will then phone me up and blame me for my choice in solicitor and the whole thing can get quite stressful.

When you use a solicitor that is recommended by the selling estate agent then it can take a lot of the stress out of the process. The estate agent cannot blame you for your choice of solicitor as they recommended them to you, in fact you can blame the estate agent if your solicitor is being slow since they gave you the recommendation. Also because the estate agent and your solicitor will have a relationship, they can communicate directly without using you as a middleman.

In short, using the solicitor recommended by the estate agent can help the conveyancing go more smoothly. However do not use their solicitor automatically without doing a bit of research. If they are unusually expensive or if they are getting bad reviews then go elsewhere. While it can certainly be useful to use them, it must always be your decision which solicitor you use, and you must always be comfortable with your decision.

Whenever I buy a property I have a set list of questions that I ask my solicitor to ensure that he considers the important issues. I recommend that you ask these questions to your solicitor.

- Are there any problems with letting? Consider my example above where a property I almost purchased would not allow me to let out to a tenant.

- Are there any restrictions on modifying the apartment? For example if I want to knock a wall down (not that I have ever done this but it's good to know).

- What are the rights of way? Is there is a path at the back that I can use?

A good solicitor that understands property investing will already consider these issues but it doesn't hurt to ask these things. Buying a property is a serious business and you don't want to leave anything to chance.

CHAPTER 10 - HOW TO REFURBISH

In our house, we almost always have the property channel on. It is one of the few things on TV that my wife and I can agree on. I especially like the programmes where people are looking for properties to buy and then have to choose one from all that they have seen. I prefer these programmes because this is my favourite part of the process when I buy a house for myself – I like to look around several properties and then make a decision based on all the information I have.

My wife however prefers the programmes where they refurbish a house and take it from a hovel to something that looks quite nice. I think this is because women are more creative than men and so they like to imagine what they can do with a house. If you are a creative person then the chances are you will also like the idea of refurbishing a property.

However, you do not need to be creative when it comes to refurbishing your property. In fact – being creative may actually be a hindrance. Like in every other step in this book – you need to follow a clear set of rules.

You are buying the property as an investment, and as such, you will not be living there. Forget please, any ideas you might have of turning your 1 bedroom flat into your own personal mini-paradise. One person's meat is another person's poison and although you may love how your property now looks, any potential tenant may not.

Essentials

Before we get into the design side of things though, we had better cover the essentials. These are things that you must attend to – failure to do so could mean you get sued over even go to prison!!

The Electrics – The electrics in any property must be safe to use and as the landlord you are responsible for this. These days you must use a qualified electrician to carry out any major electrical work. To find such an electrician, try this website (www.niceic.org.uk) which is the website for the National Inspection Council for Electrical Installation.

Fire Safety – If your property is furnished then you must ensure that the furniture is properly labeled. I strongly recommend that you let out your house unfurnished for this and many other reasons. I would also recommend installing smoke alarms in your property if there are none currently installed (if the property was built after 1992 then there is a legal requirement for installation). Get more information here: www.firekills.co.uk

Gas – All appliances that use Gas must be checked on an annual basis by a CORGI registered tradesperson. These checks need to be in place for you to legally rent out your property. To find a CORGI registrant, go to this website – www.trustcorgi.com

Fixing things

Okay, so what are the rules when it comes to the non-essentials? First and foremost – only pay for something to be done to your flat, if the cost of doing so is less than the increased value that this will add to your property. This is the case for fixing things – if you have to fix a broken tap then this will add more value to your property than the cost of getting it fixed. Your tenant will want everything in good working order so fix (or arrange to be fixed) anything that has broken.

If you have a kitchen that doesn't look atrocious then leave it alone. Some people may disagree with me on this and they are entitled to – but from my experience tenants will want something is practical and as long as you follow the guidelines contained in this chapter then that is enough for most people. Don't go crazy in other words.

When it comes to kitchens and bathrooms my main concern is plugging any leaks. In my first apartment that I bought, there was a gap between the bath and the wall and so water was seeping through. The problem came to ahead when it started to rain dirty bath water on the apartment below. Because I had a letting agent and because it was really the freeholder's problem, this wasn't too much of a headache for me. My letting agent organised temporary accommodation for my tenant and the freeholder arranged somebody to come in and fix the problem. Anyway, the point is, I could have saved my tenant (and the poor person in the flat below) some trouble if I had ensured that there was no such gap that water could seep into. Ever since then, this is I something I do look at.

I should mention here that once you rent out a property, you are responsible for fixing anything that was in the property when the tenant moved in. If you have a working microwave in the property when the tenant moves in then you have a responsibility to ensure that you provide a tenant with a working microwave for the period of their tenancy.

It might even be argued that if you have a non-working microwave in the property when a tenant moves in, that you may have to fix it and provide a tenant with a working microwave for the period of their tenancy. An inventory is normally undertaken by the letting agent prior to a tenant moving in and this involves a (junior) member of the letting agent staff walking around the flat and making a list of everything contained therein. If he spots a microwave then he will include this on the list and there is a good chance that he will not check to see if it works. The list will therefore contain "microwave" and the tenant will therefore expect a working microwave. The fewer electrical appliances you have, the better as there as less things that you need to be responsible for.

On one property I was renting out, the letting agent found a packet of Soy Sauce in one of the cupboards and then added this to the inventory. Thankfully the tenant spotted this and successfully argued that it should be taken off.

Personally I want as little in the flat as possible when I rent them out. The property will be empty apart from

- Sinks

- Bath/shower

- Toilet

- Curtain rails

- Kitchen unit

If there are any large items like a washing machine, or a fridge in the property when I buy them, then I will leave them in there as long as they are in good working order. Anything else like a kettle or a microwave will get chucked out. It's a good idea to make sure that there are no appliances left in a cupboard before you rent out your property as you will be responsible for it.

Walls and Carpets

In my mind, the most important aspect of refurbishing (along with fixing things) is taking care of the walls and carpets. This is the other area where you can greatly increase the value of your property for a relatively small cost. I will arrange for the walls to be repainted and lay new carpets about 95% of the time. The only occasion where I will not do this is where the condition of the walls & carpet is so good anyway when I bought the place that I cannot justify the extra expenditure of getting it redone (the cost will be more than the increased value a new cost of paint and carpet will provide). This part of the refurbishment adds so much value to your property - if you get it done right.

What do I mean by getting it done right? By this I mean you have <u>neutral</u> colours on the walls and on the floor – and nothing else. Perhaps purple is your favourite colour and you wish the entire apartment to be coloured purple. You need to remember though, what you like is quite frankly, irrelevant.

Neutral is the key word here. I can't stress this enough. You want your property to be nice and clean and have neutral colours throughout. This means that the walls should be white/cream, and the carpets should be a light colour – white/cream is fine here also but I tend to go for a very light brown as it also neutral.

A lot of people trip up during the refurbishment phase because they refuse to follow this simple rule – despite the fact that this is the one thing that all experienced investors agree on. I'm not saying use neutral colours because I like to see neutral colours in an apartment. I'm not saying use neutral colours because all the property experts say you should use neutral colours. I am saying neutral colours because this is what the VAST MAJORITY of potential tenants want to see when they view your property. I hope that puts to rest any ideas that you may have of decorating the apartment in your football team colours or other such nonsense.

Costing the Refurbishment

Here's a question for you. When do you cost the refurbishment? (i.e. when do you assess what needs to be done and how much it will cost you) Is it after you have bought the property but before then tenant has moved in? No. You cost the refurbishment before you purchase it – you cost it the very first time you view the property with the estate agent. The reason you do it before you purchase is so that if anything major needs done such replacing the entire kitchen or bathroom then you will want to factor that in when evaluating the deal.

The cost of refurbishing will obviously vary depending on the size of the property and the state of repair it is in. The following is a guide though based on my experiences with 1 bedroom flats.

Essentials (this is what I budget for if the walls and carpets are fine as they are and don't need replacing):

Electrics - £600

Cleaning - £100

Gas & Boiler Maintenance - £100

Carpets - £800

Painting - £800

Let us add a contingency amount of £400 to take the total budget up to £2,800.

Most of the time though I need to get a new kitchen or bathroom if they existing ones are in a state of disrepair (and so the cost to replace would be less than the increased value to the property).

If this is the case I will budget another £800 for the kitchen and £600 for the bathroom. So if a property needed both these rooms done, the total I will budget for is £4,400 (£2,800 as above plus £800 for the kitchen and £600 plus another contingency of £200 for the kitchen and bathroom).

Builders

If you are like me, then you will not like doing DIY. If you are very like me, then you will hate it. Being an accountant by trade, I've never been good with my hands and can't stand manual labour. Fortunately for me though, there are many people out there who are very good at this kind of work, and their services can be obtained for a reasonable price if you do your research.

The best place to look is in the classified section of the local newspaper. See if there is anyone offering their services. Another good source is your letting agent (which we will discuss in the next chapter) – ask them if they know of any good builders in the area. The yellow pages or other phone directory is another good source of local builders – try looking under builders.

The following websites may also help in sourcing a good builder.

www.paintingdecoratingassociation.net

www.fmb.org.uk

www.buildersguild.co.uk

www.builders.org.uk

When dealing with builders, it is very important that you draw up a contract. This can save you countless hours in arguing over some misunderstanding and could even save you going to court. A contract does not need to be complicated it just needs to cover the following points:

- The amount to be paid to the builder

- A stipulation that the builder must advise you if there are going to be cost overruns.

- Start and finish dates

- A detailed description of the work that the builder will perform.

- Dispute resolution – how any disagreements will be resolved.

- When the builder expects to complete his work

One thing I should probably mention here, always make sure that you pay (and put in the contract) a fixed fee for the work done. Some builders like to be paid an hourly rate which means there is no incentive for them to complete the work quickly. You will be paying them for their extended toilet and snack breaks. If they insist on being paid on an hourly rate then tell them you will need to find someone else to do the work – trust me, you will not get a good deal by going down the hourly rate route.

Make sure that you inspect the builder's work prior to the due completion date – say a day or 2 before. This is where you will put together your snagging list. A snagging list is a list of items that you think still need attention such as an area of the wall that needs a bit more paint or a sticking up bit of carpet. You would write all such items down on your snagging list and then ask the builder to make sure that these items have been addressed in order to complete the work to your satisfaction. As long as you use common sense and are reasonable then the builder will likely also be reasonable and attend to your items. Asking him to cut off a tiny part of carpet that is sticking up is probably unreasonable but if it is large enough that you notice it as soon as walk in the room then it would be reasonable to ask him to sort it out.

I have one more thing to say on builders and it is quite important, especially if you are buying several properties in the area, and that is – pay the builders as soon as they have finished the work. Its sounds like common sense but so many of us delay our payments and this is one case where it can be very beneficial to pay promptly. If you pay promptly then the builder may work harder and faster for you next time. It also means that if he has a busy schedule he will prioritise your job before others.

So once you are satisfied that he completed the work (including everything on your snagging list) then write him a cheque there and then.

CHAPTER 11 - HOW TO MANAGE YOUR PROPERTY

Use letting agents or manage the property yourself?

Once a property has been purchased and the first time landlord is about to rent out the property – they almost always ask themselves the big question – do they let this out themselves or do they find a letting agent?

As far as I am concerned the answer is simple – ALWAYS USE A LETTING AGENT.

I received an email yesterday from the property manager of a building where one of my flats is located telling me that my flat is leaking water from my property onto the property underneath and that I must contact them IMMEDIATELY. My response to them was this – "You should not be contacting me with matters such as this – you have my letting agent's details so please contact them". I then went and enjoyed a long walk without a care in the world. If I did not have a letting agent then I would be scrambling around trying to find a plumber, trying to get in contact with my tenant to give access to the plumber etc. etc. The fact is I am far too lazy to want to anything like this – I want to enjoy my life.

The more properties you have then the more likely that these kind of problems will occur, and some problems can be very bad indeed. I have heard stories of tenants assaulting their landlords, refusing to move out and not paying rent. The list is endless. I do not wish to lie awake at night and worry about problems I have with my tenants and I don't have to. I have hired a very competent letting agent to do this work for me.

Managing the Property

A good letting agent will perform the following tasks when looking after your property. When going through this list, think of all the hassle this would cause you if you were to look after this yourself:

- Carry out reference checks on your tenants before they sign the lease;

- Prepare the Assured Shorthold Tenancy Agreement;

- Set up a standing order to collect the rent;

- Prepare an inventory of all the items included in the property;

- Issue tenant with legal notices if required;

- Inspect the property regularly;

- Deal with maintenance issues on your behalf (this is the real timesaver).

Finding a tenant

A letting agent will help you find a tenant for your property. Getting the right tenant in can be a laborious process and without a letting agent you will need to show people around the property yourself. Sometimes many viewings are required before a property is let so this will cut into your personal time. A tenant might also move out after 6 months or a year so you will have to repeat the process again and again – for all the properties that you own. I am sure you have better things to do – leave this to the professionals.

A good letting agent will do the following for you to help sure your property gets let out:

- Put a "To Let" sign on the property;

- Take out large advertisements in local property newspapers;

- Show prospective tenants around your property;

- Text and/or email suitable tenants that they have on their books;

- Advertise on their website;

- Advertise on other popular websites such as Rightmove and Zoopla.

Selecting a Letting Agent

So let us take it as read that you now know you will need a letting agent. The next big question that people ask is "How much should I pay for a letting agent?" The answer to do this seems to be dictated by the market and by Geography so that the going rate in one part of the country at a particular point in time maybe very different to another location at another point in time.

Right now I am paying my letting agent 10% of my monthly rental income for all my properties. Personally I think this is excellent value for money and I don't grudge paying it at all. They do so much work for me that I would happily pay much more than this. To be honest I would be happy to pay double. Not that I would though as the market dictates that the rate should be about 10% - 12% in my area. You will be able to find a good letting agent for 15% or less in your chosen area.

There are some other factors that you need to consider in your letting agent besides price so I will talk about that now.

Size. When it comes to letting agents then I believe that size does matter - especially as you grow your portfolio as you will want them to look after all your properties. In order to handle my portfolio, my letting agent needs to be of a certain size.

Also a larger company can benefit from economies of scale which keeps their costs down and ultimately the cost to you as their customer. Large supermarkets like Asda and Tesco leverage their size to lower their costs and hence their prices. Compare the price of baked beans at Asda to your local corner shop and you will see what I am on about here. The point I am making is that larger companies can provide services to you more cheaply so that you either pay less for a given service or you enjoy better service at any given price.

To get an idea of who the big players are in your market – go onto the Rightmove website and look at one bedroom properties for rent. Look to see who the letting agents are for these properties and shortlist those whose names pop up frequently.

In most areas there are plenty of competition when it comes to letting agents. If you find that the letting agent you are currently using is not delivering then move to another one. I like my letting agents to know that I have many properties and that I can use them or a number of other letting agents to manage my property. Once they know that this is the case they are more likely to look after me (and my tenants) better.

One more thing I will say about letting agents is this – make sure they are registered with the Association of Residential Letting Agents (ARLA). The ARLA is the UK's professional body for the letting agency industry. Members of this agency have to abide by a certain set of standards and if they fall short – then you can complain about

74

them to the agency. If your complaint is upheld then there are numerous sanctions that the ARLA can take. They are there to protect your interests and to make sure that you don't get ripped off. Also ARLA letting agents are insured against fraud and bankruptcy which means you will receive the rents owed to you if the letting agent acts fraudulently or goes out of business. Have a look at the ARLA website - www.arla.co.uk/

I heard a story from a "property expert" who preached that it did not matter whether you used an ARLA registered letting agent or not. The last I heard about this man, the letting agent ran off with his tenants money so the mortgage was unable to be paid and it looked like the property was about to be repossessed. I never did find out what happened next but the point is it is very unlikely that the letting agents were registered with the ARLA. It matters a great deal therefore that your chosen letting agent has this designation.

CHAPTER 12 - THE STRATEGY

There must be hundreds or even thousands of different property investment strategies being used by investors in the UK. These strategies might involve buying only a certain type of property or buying in a certain area. It might involve buying, holding for a few years and then selling. You get the picture – there are loads of different strategies. Some are better than others.

This whole book covers my strategy, which involves purchasing one bedroom flats in seaside towns, not too far from a railway station. If I had to sum up what I have covered so far in one sentence then that would be it.

There is a bit more to my strategy than that though and this is what I am going to cover in this final chapter.

The Strategy

You will likely understand by now, how much I love property and how great I think it is, as an investment. I will continue to buy properties for as long as I can – I really don't believe that I can have too many. I love to watch my portfolio of properties grow and look forward to increasing the size of this portfolio.

When I was a child, my mother was fond of telling me that "money doesn't grow on trees". The funny thing is, this is exactly what I view a property as – a tree with money for leaves. Each year, as the tree grows (the property value increases) the more leaves there are. Through refinancing (which I will talk about in a bit) I am able to gather up these leaves and take them home with me. Sorry for the analogy but I think it helps get my point across.

It is therefore in my interest to have as many of these trees as possible – wouldn't you agree? If there really was such a thing as money growing trees, would you not want as many trees as possible? I would. Would you ever cut these trees down? I certainly wouldn't. This is why I am surprised when property investors sell their properties. I see it on those lunchtime TV programmes all the time. Quite often they showcase somebody who bought a dump for cheap, did it up, and then sold it for a profit. The presenter of the programme will then shake the investors hand and there are beaming smiles all around. I am left shaking my head and thinking "Why didn't you rent it out so you can keep ownership of this nice place and still make an income on it". Granted, it's not a one bedroom flat so it will be harder to rent but still.

Anyway, it's not really for me to question other people's strategies and if they are happy then fine. Besides which I need people to sell or I would have nobody to buy from. I would never ever sell myself though. I would never cut down one of my trees for a quick profit. Analogy over, I promise.

But I hope I have made my point. When you buy a house it should be like when you buy a puppy and be a lifetime commitment. I don't believe you should ever sell. As long as property prices go up over the long term (as they always have done) then you will continue to make money from your property.

So what is my strategy then? How can I capitalize on the fact that my property is going up in value if I never sell. The answer is, I refinance. Refinancing is where you obtain a new mortgage based on the current value of your property (which should have appreciated from when you bought the property). With this new mortgage, you will be able to pay off your old one and still have plenty of money left over.

So let's say, you purchased a property three years ago for £70,000 when the market price for the property was £100,000. The market price (based on the asking prices for comparable nearby properties) is now £110,000. Let us also assume that you obtained a mortgage for 80% LTV for both the original mortgage and your remortgage.

The original loan amount was (£70,000 * 80%) = £56,000

The second mortgage is (£110,000 * 80%) = £88,000

So when the lender gives you a cash sum of £88,000 during the refinancing, you will pay off the original mortgage of £56,000 and the balance of £32,000 (£88,000 – £56,000) is yours. Not bad is it?

The Process

So here is what to do. Let as assume you have just bought a property and are in the process of getting it refurbished. Let us also assume that the mortgage product you have obtained for the original purchase of the property allows you to pay back the entire mortgage after 6 months (currently, most mortgages will try and tie in you for a few years, and you will have to pay a penalty to make early repayments but we'll come back to this later).

So whilst the flat is getting refurbished you approach your mortgage broker and solicitor and tell them that you want to remortgage your property. You will provide your mortgage broker and solicitor with all the information they require (as you did for your original mortgage).

Your mortgage broker will recommend you with a 2nd lender. This new lender will arrange for an independent surveyor to come in and value your property (by then, hopefully the refurbishment will have completed), and the amount of money that the new lender will give to you depends on what the surveyor thinks your property is worth. This point is key.

If you have bought wisely then this new amount to be lent to you (which we call the revaluation amount) will already be way above your original purchase price since you will have bought BMV. The fact that your property will be newly refurbished with neutral colours will also tend to push the value up in the surveyor's mind. The surveyor should come in with a value well in excess of what you paid for the flat. In the example above which I think is very realistic – I would receive excess cash of £32,000. I will use this as a deposit for my next property which will allow me to grow my portfolio, I will then revalue this property, receive more cash, put down a deposit for yet another property and so on and so on and so on.

I said above that the surveyor should come in with a value well in excess of what you paid for the flat. It would be wrong to assume that the surveyor will always come in with your expected value. The surveyor might be in a bad mood that day, they may be incompetent or they might just not like you. The fact is though the surveyor is human and is prone to the same failings as the rest of us. In those (hopefully rare) situations where the revaluation comes up short – the best thing to do is just accept it and look ahead to your next property. By accepting it though, it doesn't mean you shouldn't read his report to try and understand why the revaluation was lower than expected. It could be that there is a very good reason why the value is low – perhaps something you missed. If this is the case, then it is important that you learn from this for when you make your future purchases.

I mentioned above that mortgages may try and tie you in for a few years and you may have to pay a penalty if you remortgage within a given time period. Unfortunately this is just the current state of the credit market in the UK where lenders are being very restrictive when it comes to terms on the mortgages they offer. If you wish to remortgage as soon as possible then you may have to factor in the penalty you will have to pay to your initial lender as part of your refinancing costs.

You don't have to refinance straight away though and it is perfectly acceptable to buy a property, get some tenants in for a few years, get it refurbished, and then do the refinance. It really depends on how aggressive you are as an investor and how much you feel you can get your property revalued for (based on the comparable properties). Right now across most of the UK, property prices are quite stagnant and have been for several years. It may take some time before we see property prices rising again. If you have bought well below BMV (and you should have if you followed the guidelines in this book) then the market value of your property is already well above what you paid for it so you can realize this amount by refinancing.

Getting all your money out

When I buy a property, it is my aim to get all my money out when I refinance. To explain what I mean by getting all my money out, let us look again at the example I used above whereby a property was purchased for £70,000 three years ago with an 80% LTV mortgage, and then refinanced with a new value of £110,000.

The original loan amount was (£70,000 * 80%) = £56,000

The second mortgage is (£110,000 * 80%) = £88,000

Remember the surplus you will receive from this refinance is £32,000 (£88,000 – £56,000). This is £32,000 cash in your hand you have from doing this refinance.

Let us now have a look at your total outgoings when purchasing this property.

The most obvious outgoing is the deposit you paid on your first mortgage three years ago. Since the purchase price was £70,000 and the mortgage was 80% LTV, you had to pay the 20% deposit:

£70,000 * 20% = £14,000.

Let us assume that you paid solicitors fees of approximately £1,000 and mortgage brokerage fees of £500. These are realistic estimates for such fees.

Assume also that you had to spend £4,400 on refurbishment costs.

When you arrange the revaluation you will have some additional costs to pay. As well as paying more fees to your solicitor for arranging the revaluation, you will also have to pay valuation fees for when the surveyor revalues your house. Let us assume these fees are £500 and £400 respectively.

I also like to factor in a £1,000 contingency fee to take care of any unexpected costs that may arise during the whole process.

Your total outlay is therefore:

Deposit - £14,000

Solicitor – 1st fee - £1,000

Mortgage Broker - £500

Refurbishment - £4,400

Solicitor – 2nd fee - £500

Valuation fee - £400

Contingency - £1,000

This gives us a total of £21,800

So if we received £32,000 from our revaluation but we had outgoings totaling £21,800 then we have been able to get all our money out PLUS £10,200 (£32,000 – £21,800).

You should do these calculations before your initial purchase of the property, as it is a good way of evaluating different properties and seeing where you can draw the most money from. You can use the tools I have shown you in chapters 4 and 5 to estimate what the property is worth when you do the revaluation as this is key to making this process work.

However, you don't have to be able to get all your money out of a property in this way for it still to be a worthwhile deal. All property goes up in value in the long term and so all property should make you money in the long term. However if you are able to calculate that you will be able to get all your money out, then it gives you added confidence that your investment is a sound one.

Several people have emailed me to ask why I just wouldn't sell the properties instead of remortgaging them. The answer is simply:

(i)   I want to avoid the tax consequences of selling. You would get a large tax bill from any capital gains you made on this property once you sell.

(ii)   I want to continue to own the property so that I can continue to get money from it year after year after year. When you sell a property you can get money from the sale but then that's it. The property you sold will never give you a penny more once you stop owning it.

If I can just convince you that buying and selling properties is not the thing to do then you will have gotten far more than your money's worth from this book. Continuing to own the property whilst occasionally refinancing is the way to get ahead in this business.

SO WHAT NOW...

So what now for you? Hopefully you will be inspired to take action and buy some property. Throughout this book I have endeavored to give you confidence to go out and there and take action. That is why I did the walkthrough on finding properties as this seems to be the big stumbling block.

There is no greater advice that I can give to you than TAKE ACTION. You will not wake up some day a millionaire without taking action. You will not wake up some day financially free without taking action. So you must take action.

Taking action does not have to be difficult. As I have shown on this book, you can take 90% of the action needed to become a successful property investor by just sitting at your computer. You just need to be persistent in taking action.

I mentioned in the introduction that you only need 5 properties to become financially free. How did I calculate this? Well according to house price surveys, such as those carried out by Halifax, Nationwide and the Land Registry, house prices increased in value in excess of 7% a year on average since the late 1960s. For simplicity, let us say that the average fair value of a 1 bedroom apartment is currently £100,000. If the price were to increase by 7% in 1 years time then the value of the property would increase be £107,000. You can get a hold of this extra £7,000 by using the refinancing techniques I talked about in the previous chapter.

So if we had 5 properties valued at £100,000 each and they all increased by 7% then what would the total value of our portfolio be? Well a portfolio of £500,000 (5 * £100,000) would increase by £35,000 over a year if the property appreciated by 7%. Even minus the transaction costs an amount of £35,000 received on average each year would be higher than the current average wage in the UK. Even if we are conservative and say that property will appreciate by only 5% in a year, well that is still an increase of £25,000. More than enough I am sure to pay your bills, food and other living expenses and still have plenty left over to enjoy life. And if you need/want more than that then just buy more properties!!!

Of course property will not appreciate by 5% or 7% every year and in some years it will not appreciate at all but what we are looking at here is averages and on average it has gone up in excess of 7% in the past. I see no reason to believe that it will not continue to do so in the future.

So please go out there, take action and become financially free.

I would love to hear your success stories in your property investing business. Please let me know how you get on at http://propertyinvestinguk.com/contact-us/

So what now for me? Well I will be continuing to purchase properties of course and will do so forever.

I have now set up my membership site: http://propertyinvestinguk.com/. On this site I find and recommend for consideration more than 100 possible BMV deals in different seaside locations around the UK. I have also included the calculator I use to analyse my deals to see if I can get all my money out based on the maths I described in chapter 12. I also include an extremely large resources section with links to over 70 websites which will aid you in meeting your property investment goals.

To help me in future book revisions, please let me know what you thought of this book. Is there anything you particularly liked or didn't like? Is there anything you feel that I need to expand on or provide more clarity on? If so then please email me, the address again is http://propertyinvestinguk.com/contact-us/.

Until next time, I wish you success in your new property investing business. Please remember to review this book on Amazon. Thank you very much!!

GLOSSARY

Assured Shorthold Tenancy Agreement:

This is the default residential tenancy agreement in England and Wales and is the most common form of arrangement involving a private residential landlord. The equivalent in Scotland is the Short Assured Tenancy Agreement.

Base Rate:

The Bank of England interest rate which lenders use as the base for the interest rate they set on their mortgage products.

Break Clause:

A clause interested into an agreement which allows the landlord or tenant to break the contract under certain conditions.

Bridging Loan:

A short term loan taken out whilst awaiting longer term financing and serves as an interim arrangement. More expensive than conventional financing to compensate for the additional risk of the loan.

Building Regulations:

Statutory regulations that seek to ensure that relevant legislation is carried out in relation to any building developments.

Buildings Insurance:

Insurance taken out to cover the fixtures and fittings within a property.

Buy To Let:

The purchase of a property where the intention is to let this property out to a third party.

Buy To Let Mortgage:

An arrangement in which an investor borrows money to purchase property in the private rented sector in order to let it out to tenants. Buy To Let Mortgages have been on offer in the UK since the late 1990s.

Buying Off Plan:

Buying property which has yet to be constructed.

Capital Gains Tax:

A tax on the profit realised on the sale of property, where the property was purchased at a cost amount lower than the amount realised on the sale.

Capital Growth:

The increase in value of a certain property over a certain period of time.

Distressed Seller:

A seller who has motivation to sell quickly and for a price below market value, usually due to their own cash flow concerns.

Equity:

The ownership interest in a property calculated by taking the price paid for a property minus the mortgage.

Exchange Of Contracts:

An exchange of contracts occurs after a solicitor has carried out all necessary searches and there is agreement to the contract terms. Once each party has signed the contracts and they have been exchanged, they are binding.

Final Sale Price:

The price of the property agreed to be paid when the contracts are exchanged.

Fixed Rate Mortgage:

A mortgage where the interest rate does not fluctuate during the fixed rate period of the loan. This allows the borrower to accurately predict their future payments.

Flipping:

The process where a property is bought and then resold for a profit, usually over a short amount of time.

Forfeiture:

A clause in a rental agreement which gives the landlord powers to evict a tenant.

Freehold:

Full ownership of property. This is opposed to a **leasehold** where the property reverts to the owner of the land after the leasehold has expired.

Ground Rent:

A regular payment made by the owner of a leasehold property to the freeholder, as required under the lease.

House Price Index:

An index that measures the price of residential housing. The indexes provided by the HM Land Registry, Halifax and Nationwide are the most well know indexes in the UK.

IFA:

Independent Financial Adviser. Professionals who offer independent advice on financial matters to their clients and recommend suitable financial products from the whole of the market. Such products include mortgages.

Inheritance Tax:

A levy paid by a person who inherits property or a tax on the estate (which includes any property) of a person who has died.

Interest Only Mortgage:

A mortgage where the borrower only pays the interest on the principal balance, with the principal balance being unchanged. At the end of the mortgage term, the borrower must pay back the entire amount of the principal balance.

Leasehold:

A right to hold title to property for a given length of time. A leasehold differs from a **freehold** where the ownership of a property is purchased outright and also differs from a tenancy where a property is let out on a periodic basis such as monthly or yearly.

Local Searches:

A search on matters pertaining on a property that can be obtained from local authorities.

Mortgage:

In this context, a mortgage is a loan secured on property with the proceeds of the loan being used to purchase this property.

Mortgage Agreement In Principle:

Where a lender agrees to provide a loan to a borrower on a property subject to the lender's verification of the borrower's and the property's details.

Mortgage Protection Policy:

An insurance policy that will meet mortgage obligations if the borrower dies or becomes unwell.

Repayment Mortgage:

A mortgage in which the monthly repayments consist of repaying the capital amount borrowed as well as the accrued interest, so that the amount borrowed decreases throughout the term and by the end of the loan term, has been fully repaid. This contracts with an **Interest Only Mortgage.**

Sealed Bid:

This is a form of auction, where bidders submit one bid in a concealed fashion and where the person with the highest bid being awarded the property. This person would then pay his bid to the seller.

Shared Ownership:

This allows a person to purchase a share in their own home, even if they cannot afford a mortgage on the whole of the current value. The remaining equity share may be held by the house developer, by a private investor or by a landlord such as a housing association. In some models the resident pays rent on that share.

Snagging:

This is a term widely used with the construction industry to describe the process of resolving defects.

Stamp Duty Land Tax:

Introduced in 2003, it is a form of self-assessed transfer tax charged on land and property transactions. Currently 0% for all residential UK property purchases up to £125,000.

Survey:

An inspection on the condition of a property.

Title Deeds:

Documents showing ownership, as well as rights, obligations, or mortgages on a property.

Vacant Possession:

Property law concept that refers to a legal obligation to ensure that a property is in a state fit to be occupied at a given point in time.

Variable Rate:

Where the interest rate will fluctuate based on the Bank of England **base rate**. This is opposed to a **Fixed Rate Mortgage.**

Void:

The period when a property is vacant and thus is not receiving rental income from a tenant.

Yield:

In the context, of the buy to let strategy, this is the amount of annual rental income on a property relevant to the purchase price of the property.

15184913R00055

Printed in Poland
by Amazon Fulfillment
Poland Sp. z o.o., Wrocław